The Goats Have Taken Over The Barracks

poems by

Andrew Najberg

Finishing Line Press
Georgetown, Kentucky

The Goats Have Taken Over The Barracks

poems by

Andrew Najberg

Finishing Line Press
Georgetown, Kentucky

The Goats Have Taken Over The Barracks

ACKNOWLEDGMENTS

"1st Island Fisherman Mending His Nets" first appeared in *Bamboo Ridge Review.*

"Aeration" first appeared in *Istanbul Review.*

"A Murder of Eels" first appeared in *New Millennium Writings.*

"At the Center of it" first appeared in *Another Chicago Magazine*

"Frozen Pond" first appeared in *Istanbul Review.*

"Getting it Right" first appeared in *Nashville Review.*

"The goats have taken over the barracks" first appeared in *Artful Dodge.*

"Godwin's Law" first appeared in *Yemassee*

"Grandfather" first appeared in *Louisville Review.*

"Grasping Dust" first appeared in *Cimarron Review.*

"Hearing the cuckoos cry" first appeared in *Outscape*

"Hydration is of the Essence" first appeared in *Yemassee.*

"The Last Note" first appeared in *Bat City Review*

"Listening to Doors" first appeared in *Louisville Review.*

"Ouroboros" first appeared in *Blood and Thunder*

"Reverence" first appeared in *North American Review.*

"Stroke Vigil" first appeared in *Another Chicago Magazine*

"Waiting for Her Surgery" first appeared in *Blood and Thunder*

Publisher: Leah Huete de Maines
Editor: Christen Kincaid
Cover Art: Andrew Najberg
Author Photo: Amber Danielle Najberg
Cover Design: Elizabeth Maines McCleavy

Order online: www.finishinglinepress.com
also available on amazon.com

Author inquiries and mail orders:
Finishing Line Press
P. O. Box 1626
Georgetown, Kentucky 40324
U. S. A.

Table of Contents

Dedicated To
Amber, Gillian, and Elliott

I.

Blind Equation

The watch back gleamed silver under
slow rotating ceiling fan blades
that disturbed the room currents,

parts sprawled across the coffee table,
my young mind with no account or catalogue
whether all still remained.

I vained to reconfigure the tiny
cogs with a jewelry screwdriver
and needle tweezers,

now a matter of time before my mother
returned home from work and discovered
what I'd done to my Christmas gift.

I still regard as somewhat magical
mechanical watches
regardless of understanding the principles

that drive hands across their faces,
knowing my own hands jitter
too much to attempt any such repair.

I don't remember my physics well,
but the motion of all those
intricate gears can be explained

in an equation or two, a simple matter
of ratios, mechanical advantage,
and the force exerted by a little wound spring.

How much like the mother at the aisle's end now,
head hung over the tiny coffin amid all those
luminous flowers and wreaths,

she winds her spring so tight that the blades

of her back pitch up her black dress like tents,
a hollow valley where her spine should pole,

she holds her hands to her face,
until her fingers set in motion,
crawl her skin in millimeters.

The tips grope down her neck and shoulders,
down the fabric that shimmers like velour
in the church lights, until they depart

to the varnished wood, lacquer so thick
the child could be buried in its shape alone.
She ticks her nails into each groove and seam

as if the right purchase will take a tomb apart,
deconstruct death into component parts
to be extracted piece by piece

like dust from each strand of her daughter's hair,
from the little creases in her lips, the little fold
of baby fat under her chin.

Ouroboros

The worst thing about when the bottom of a full, five gallon jug ruptures
on your kitchen tile is the moment of complete helplessness

as you watch water flow down grout channels
and in gliding liquid sheets towards the back door

because that moment becomes the instant
your chest hit the trunk of the police car,

the metal pinch on your wrists
in the excessive heat of a July Texas sun.

The rush of water soaking the stack of cookbooks
by the laundry room door becomes the night

your grandmother died 3,000 miles away
and you could not reach her.

That pool around your feet is knowing someday
your now infant daughter might lie in a hospital bed,

her lips quivering too much to sip her water glass.
It's cancer or an accident shattered her spinal column.

Maybe the doctors won't have a name for it.
There at her bedside, one hand leaning her head forward,

the other setting down the glass,
you dip a spoon in reconstituted mashed potatoes

as you recite bits of eighteen different half-remembered
bedtime stories because words should not exist for some goodbyes.

Then, once the heart monitor stands untethered and silent,
you stand too, drenched in cold sweat, socks soaked in shoes.

Grandfather

When the professor tore the readout from the dot matrix printer—
it was old fashioned because he was old fashioned—
      we knew we'd done it.

We had calculated the number of lemons
that mankind would probably consume
before the end of existence
      under current parameters.
We could finally go home.

Last week it was the number of snail shells lying empty in English garden beds,
before that the number of rain drops in a three hour storm.
      We knew the world so well.

We tabulated the number of table legs ever wrought by carpenters
and the number of the same sawed and stained by furniture factories.
      We even knew the number of tears it would take to fill the pacific ocean
      depending on whether the criers were infants, girls under 10,
      professional football players or widows.

This is exactly how much you cried when your husband died, we could tell them.
      This is how many tears fell onto your husband's hand,
         and this is how many milliseconds the warmth of those tears
         forestalled the cooling of his skin.
Isn't this grand we said? Doesn't this help you with your grief, Mrs. Najberg?

But she said she didn't want to know. Just shook her head and said she didn't want
to know.
There were still pills in a plastic cup on the corner of his dinner tray
      next to the applesauce.   The napkin, soiled, crumpled in a wet little ball,
seemed like it wanted to soak in all the weight in the world, to draw in her grief
      and leave her clean.

Would you like to know how many of his cells are still alive?
But it's no use. She won't listen. Even as the nurses enter in
and the orderlies and the candy stripers and the doctors and the morticians, all of
them

absorbed in what must be done, what must be done,
almost no one hears her whisper that she can't, she can't, she can't.

Reverence

The underpass pylons bar me
from the ambulance as paramedics
hoist the covered corpse onto a stretcher,
imprison me in the want to touch the dead
by depriving me with distance.

At the morgue, he will be split
pelvis to sternum, abdomen unfurled
like moth wings. Organs removed,
labeled, weighed, recorded, a diagnostic
identity in place of a name

for the otherwise known as a John Doe,
exposure victim: middle aged male,
underweight. The mortician will orate
an autopsy walkthrough for a posterity
that doesn't exist: calm, dignified, dead.

Just like the voice of the professor
who performed my tour of the body farm
when I was seventeen. A monotone
monologue described a year of
extensive examination and documentation.

I had never seen a corpse before.
I was braced for awe. Not formaldehyde,
nor for rows of silver pins with white labels
too stiff to flutter in re-circulation drafts,
nor for breasts slit open and peeled back

from a chest split open and peeled back
to expose the rib cage, sawed open
and spread like bay doors as if to allow lungs
to breathe. Layer upon layer of deep
exposure. Blood in vials, not veins.

Emaciation that raised tendons

into tent wire to house her face,
a shadow of a face in shadows.
Studied anonymity: scalpel slits
under the eye sockets and hair line.

Sinus cavities and tooth sockets open
allow dust, microbe, penlight floods.
A little box next to a pan holding her brain,
her teeth sealed in numbered plastic bags.
Slides of skin, tissue, hair samples.

Same for the fingernails, the toenails.
Like unopened jigsaws of pure blue skies.
Too many pieces missing, those present
too similar. No trick of matching edges
could reassemble the real picture.

And so the tour ended in questions to our group
about who we were. Getting to know us around
the slab like a dinner with a Jane Doe centerpiece.
The life taken out of death. Height. Weight.
Age. And the type of shoes she wore when found.

Once her identity became statistic,
even if her liver said she was a drinker,
lungs, a smoker, no one would know
or ask her favorite blend. Or why
she drank so fast, lived, died so fast.

While the other students reached out in stutters
to touch her kidneys, spleen, gallbladder,
and register the rubbery texture of the walls
that divide us internally, I tried to wrap the skin back
over her stomach. To reattach her retinas

and imagine through her eyes a woman who watched
lazy Tennessee breezes blow Rorschachs of mist

above the waters and trudged through browning leaves.
Who walked the night riverbank to love the brush
of grass blades on the bulbs of her ankles.

Her name could have been Adele. Shelley.
Or maybe it really was Jane. Jane Donne.
Perhaps the sliver of white scar streaking
her temple came from a branch swipe
while trotting through the woods with the lover

she did her best drinking with. They plopped to dirt
between green reeds and tossed smoldering filters
into the current's ripple trickling over the rocks
as he brushed the backs of her hands
with his fingertips. There must have been

a last stroke of that lover's touch, calloused
thumbs that slipped over pebbled areoles,
the splash of their breaths in clouds
condensing between their parting lips.
Warmth, wet, glow of skin just touched.

They'd found her lying, washed up, still gazing
at a frozen moon. With the tips of their forked
index and middle fingers, they drew her eyes shut.
They always do. A sign of respect, that cutting off.
Close the mouth. Seal the body from the spirit.

Let it drift in and out of the ether at will, without
temptation. Maybe I will be sewn up at my morgue.
Kidneys, stomach, spleen, returned. Ready for a new
existence without mind or soul. My remains
might be shipped to that university. Professors

will lay me out in a field to decompose. No one
will know who I was or what I did, but my eyes
will be reopened to simulate proper conditions.

I will build a new identity of maggot bites,
rot patterns, and the leeching of bone marrow.

Kissed by bits of soil blown between my lips.
Back on the cold packed dirt. Frost will settle
in the folds of my clothes. Half-covered
by next winter's fallen leaves and wind
broken branches, I will gape up at cold

December stars and watch a woman's inverse
shadow drift towards me from a nebula
beyond Orion. Strands of hair will blow
from my shriveled scalp, tangle in withered
dandelion stems. A smell of frost and clover.

Grasping Dust

She beats the mattress on her porch with a chair leg despite her age and the heat.
It has not rained on the palms for quite some time so her roof has not leaked,
yet she knows the clouds that billow from the diamond quilting of the bed
are not the dust and sand that settled onto the flower petals and the tile.

For five years, she touched nothing of his room, didn't sweep the fingernails
from under the armoir or vacuum the hairs out of the rug. She even left
his toothbrush and razor by the sink in their little blue cup. They say
that slept on long enough a mattress contains several pounds of dead skin,

but she knows it's just a myth, knows that these types of memory
are little more than noon shadows, but she still saved this for last,

waiting for the salt to rust the rails of the garage door, for the little lizards
to find each and every tiny hole through the siding,
for the summer storms to blow the shingles loose enough,
that she simply needed someone to fix things. For repair.

The big palm in the corner of the yard hasn't had a green frond for seasons,
and she's even stopped asking the sweet young neighbor to mow the Bermuda grass.

Yes, now she has no choice but to beat a haze that she hopes will almost
shape his ghost from his old bed. Out on the porch,
she holds a wet rag up to her nose with her left hand and each blow jolts
through her bones like she awakens again and again and again.

Stroke Vigil

I'd been living alone in my two bedroom
and I'd set my palm on the stove
as I waited for my coffee to percolate,

not realizing I'd left the eye on all night,
that I'd absently set the soup pot beside the sink
after the phone rang and I heard.

Now, with a bandaged hand,
I kneel before votives in her favorite church
as she recedes in the hospital.

To my left, a child in a blue dress
lights candle after candle,
her mother in the front pew.

Wilting in her bed, my godmother
has lost all vision in one eye
and half the peripheral in the other.

They call the latter a sympathetic loss—
physiologically, there's no shorted wiring,
but we were meant to see the world with both eyes,

to clasp both hands in prayer,
and, one hand dangling by my thigh,
it strikes me that when it comes to our gods

we often hold conversations where only
the speaker listens,
and only with one ear.

Waiting for her surgery

This is how I sat, sit, hopefully will be sitting,
unyielding in an unyielding chair
that itches wherever my weight concentrates,
an itch as bad as this sitting at a bedside,

while the janitor in his gray overalls
shoves his yellow bucket past the door
by the mop handle, his breast pocket dangling
a plastic lanyard, his belt clipped with keys:

I'm upright, one foot crossed over my knee with my
jacket damp from late February rain crumpled
on the trademark institutional linoleum
behind my boot heel. A little blue duffel

tucked in the corner behind the heart monitor,
not monitoring now, I listen to charts
slide in and out of the boxes hanging outside
the doors of neighboring rooms

turning faces into names into patients into
height, weight, temperature, bpms, rpms,
diastolic over systolic, allergies, current
medications, observations, treatments in progress

and from further down the hall a rumble
of a wheeled tower of devices whose names
I don't know but the colors of whose lights
I can name with grade school accuracy

trundles towards another one to wire up,
to work up, to write up, each electronic device
ready to listen to the hearts, lungs, brains,
dying to be plugged into that purpose giving

electricity and buzz with Circadian rhythm,
like a psychoanalyst with nerve cells, muscle cells,

skin cells, t-cells, lymph cells on the couch about
to talk about their mother cells,

the one's that split wrong, that kept splitting,
spawning malformed wells of cytoplasm,
littered with mitochondria, ribosomes,
endoplasmic reticulum sipping on nucleotide soup,

or perhaps those tyrannical neurons
whose axons, dendrites, myelin sheaths, synaptic gaps
work like dirty words when they order the body to misfire,
and it's their firing that lets me listen to the scribbling EKG

and the soft rustle of its scrolling paper rumples like napkins
into its basin, a heap corrugated like the folds of the gray matter
it records, only for the confessions to end up boxed
in some basement records room with a 10 digit keypad entry,

a locked storehouse of maps of mind soon to be forgotten,
trapped in the Alzheimer's of bureaucracy only occasionally
shifted about by a technician named Wendell who carries
a Ziplocked ham and cheese sandwich in his lab coat pocket

and the photos of three different women in his back right,
who shuffles about with one shoe almost untied,
a five o'clock shadow on his chin and a hangover shadow
under his eyes regardless of the hour,

while I tap my fingers on metal arm rests, thumb
printing the shine. Immediately, I wipe away the oils
because it feels strange to dirty something in a hospital,
to be something dirty in a hospital,

while the nurse strips the sheets, crumples a great big bundle
she shoves into a cloth sack hanging from her cart.
This is the point I think that as she slips the fresh set
over the bed corners and the wafer pillows

in her mind she's tossed the coin whether she's making
the bed for someone coming back, and six floors below
Wendell scuttles off to the corner of the EKG file room
and jams a bit of chaw under his lip in a half crouch

that exposes the fraying seam in the crotch of his jeans
with the two stitches just loose enough to let an astute looker
glimpse his tighty whiteys. Wendell lets his rump fall
to the cold tile, his back against a stack of boxes

and his feet slide until splayed with bent knees.
He hooks his elbows over the caps and spits
a little pool of brown tobacco juice
just in front of his ass crack.

He knows the janitor, knows that someone will clean it up
and the next day will go on just the same.
Lucky him.

II.

Losing you

Still life with crow. Crow with still life.
Still life crow with orange blossom, vase and cheese plate.

Flock of crows, olive black eyes, feathers suspended
against sun, queued on the power line, their bread line,

watch the sidewalk lines,
flit their wings in a ripple down the row

and burst into flight at the close of your front door,
a murder of chaos at the murder of silence.

The only one that remains cocks eye down at you from the branches
of the first sycamore bare from the fall,

perhaps to your untied shoelace, that brown leather worm,
or maybe you are the worm, exposed inside and out

because she left or he died or you didn't dress your shadows
in apparel for the world and you shudder against the approaching pecking

of "I'm sorry"s and "Be strong"s,
"You just need time"—yes— time to reverse

time to take it all back to give it all back
for the linearity of experience to shove itself back up its—

your hard soles clop the walk like you're knocking on coffin wood,
too warm to thrust hands in your pockets without sweating,

your fingers bent in fists even when they're open.
When you stop at your car, listen back at the crow

as dew drips from leaves to soil, spatters a worm stranded
on a root by pre-dawn rain.

It will be dead soon, eaten or dried,
blundering its head into the hard wood gnarls.

Drop your keys jingling when the ring snags
Coins settle in your pockets as you kneel.

The bird no longer has interest in you.

Bok Crater

Once you were impact, a birth swaddled in an ejecta blanket, a twenty-seven kilometer eye open to the solar system's outer reaches.

They call your crib the dark side of the moon, but it's simply the side we never see, the one that always looks away.

And we look away too from the line between can't and won't, build telescopes and satellites and long frequency scanners to extend gaze towards celestial filaments

because there's simply too many graves to dig and our hands are made to grasp the shovel and dig but we've never been the ilk to tilt our nose toward the soil.

If our eyes could leave claw marks, the cosmos would bear deep swathes the planets could roll into like marbles as we scrawl column after column in black-bound log books, our data:

coordinates, temperatures, telemetries, radiographic magnetronic maps computer renditioning ourselves into the folds of celestial fabric.

It's not been long since our imaginations danced with the music of celestial spheres

or since we hyphenated space and time, stuck neat little hands in neat little lab coat pockets and chuckled softly before lighting our cigars.

It was and is time to clean underneath our nails.

Our glasses, smudged with sweat salt, have fallen halfway down our noses.

It doesn't matter how many of our hands don't hold a shovel.

Its only our eyes that look away.

While we gaze into the rareness of the blows that form the universe, we don't know what really defines a crater: the bowl or the space that fills it.

A hole filled with dirt is still a hole if you remember the edges.

The same of our flesh.

Hydration is of the Essence

Check if your long term plans involve life insurance.
If not, order now. Operators await

and you wait too, for the sun to rise
over the mesa and cast shadows from scorpions,

for the judgment of morning
to vex the horizon line with heat distortion.

No doubt this desert is merciless.
Even with pockets full of conviction,

body crucified by its own heat,
don't look too long at the longhorn skull.

Anywhere you rest your eyes
you don't look elsewhere.

Desert snakes strike the ankles of boots,
dig fangs into the back of knees.

You've seen shows that dramatize the anguish of the lost,
shows with titles that tell you who shouldn't survive

even though they did, even as you watch them
drag themselves parched, limped, and scorched

into a shitty little Exxon with more peel then paint
that's faded to the color of thin-blown sand

like the memories of the ones that didn't make it,
and Old Nelson behind the counter, he squints,

hovers his hand over the emergency cut-off
like he does any time anything is different.

On the counter, there's an open can of chaw,
two loser lotto tickets,

a five, three ones, two quarters,
and thirty-seven pennies from the last customer.

Sand on all the copper. One of the pumps
dangles loose from its hook like a noose.

Faith

Withering clovers gaze to the soil for drink, to the desiccated fronds and cattails, to the torn mouth of the Styrofoam cup, the Snickers wrapper stuck to the granite chunk by the fence post.

When the stream runs dry, crayfish husks under wash-round pebbles and sun-scorched eggs of water bugs thirst among brittle briar branches and crumbling skunk cabbage.

The retriever on the bank lolls tongue to the side, eyes rolled to the top, lids half shut, nostrils plugged with mucus and dust.

Kicks its ribs with ragged claws because something has found liquid beneath the skin.

In the hard packed bank, even grubs choke until they writhe from holes and dry in the sun,

and I choke too on all of it, on my knees in the crackling, snapped reeds by the dog's side.

I tilt my water bottle onto its gums and watch the water sluice through its teeth and vanish among the roots underneath and I'm not close enough to death that I don't need to gaze

to the withering clovers who don't curse the sun or the other parched grass roots or the hot winds that blow grit into the dog's teeth as they drop their leaves one by one to dirt

to add some color among all (red) their (purple) dead (orange) seeds.

Drinking coffee

Outside this cafe alone, I am always not.
Better alone than myself.

A metal table with wrought lattice top,
black and unreflective.

A knife on a napkin with no fork to love its serrations,
blade keeps the air cut in a still slit,

and I glide across the source of scars,
the only ceiling the stars,

the air unloaded as the words that fill it,
and so many empty glasses wait to be

washed and filled or not washed and filled
or not washed and not filled, until now—

Now, lemon wedge in water glass,
two seeds dig through ice cubes.

Just moments before they carve different channels.
Seeds taking root are history repeating,

so I take out my wallet
to pay for the sap and not the sapling.

Grown in pocket bottoms,
lint is a metaphor for weeping.

Porcelain is the underside
of coffee stain,

skin the underside
of atmosphere,

and all fills with swirling nimbus

rumble and flash.
Rattle of air conditioner,

of spoons in white saucers.
If you cough, I will look over to you
but nothing in either of our faces

will tell the other that we don't know
how not to overflow.

Listening to Doors

Concrete stairs to a church. Doors
wrought-iron ornamented, gilded, fading.

Is it stained glass or bas relief that panes
the paneling? Who sees through the figures

With such a stillness inside? Who is telling
the stories what they're about?

They, like me, wait
for your red coat to turn the corner.

The shops across the street are all closed
though their mannequins still parade their shawls

and the call of gulls carries from the river;
I could die among this city's

colonnades of chimneys
and rust-hampered hinges down narrow brick alleys

that caw to the ravens perched on the aerials,
sooty feathers flitter over wobbling aluminum perches,

beaks who's squawks sound like "help"
and somehow I know they won't get it.

Watching the Funnel in the East Texas Empty

Pulled off the highway a long view from Longview,
a stretch of turbulent tendon, a strained sinew of sky,

threaded down from bulging muscle cloud fibers
to the smooth stomach bulge of a horizon hilltop

only visible when the stratosphere threw down
the lightning roots of an electric naked branched elm

into the soil, the bucking funnel fulminating thunderheads
of dirt clods, scrub brush, and tree trunks

against the liminal lips of the vanishing point seam
that swallowed my perception of the world

and sealed off the bubble of my mind,
the fragile framed wobble of awareness.

I can't say I was particularly close, a couple miles away,
in a closed car with windows I kept trying to roll up

higher than they can roll, but I was far enough
that I couldn't hear the rumble and churn

of the hilltop stripping the muscle from under its skin,
the shudder in that reverse cascade of rock and loam,

the vomiting earth a silent film cast black and white
by the violence of light and shadow,

lit and unlit to the limit of which I could perceive
the difference, the only things positioned to intervene

a little distance, a pane of glass, and a single Holstein cow
in the field thrashing against a length of broken fence.

Frozen Pond

I've crouched here so long the snow on the shore lies unbroken.

Below,
angled cracks in water shelves, layers of frozen dominos.

There is silence and the sound of silent things falling.
I trace the memory of ice skates on the surface.

Somewhere underneath, the fish; somewhere the frogs survive.

Deep ice moans in gravel crunches, chafes jagged black
edges.

I am water too, but it's easy to forget
because I call myself by the flotsam suspended in it.

Without rocks to break the surface, water lies about its motion
by reflecting

the frozen pines, the late birds, and all my faces.

If the clouds were real I'd stick my hands into them
regardless of how blue my nails got.

Fingers can't trace our real edges anyway.

We all forgot the Braille of memory when our hearts began to beat.

The fractures grope numb
as ice sheets buck slow against each other,

as tectonic winter plates
shatter and rise.

Water at 34 degrees

Chill so deep cold gnaws rather than bites.

On the roadside by my car,
frost diamonds an unfortunate squirrel.

Perhaps it was the expansion of water
freezing within its body

or the simple pressure
of the tire that killed it,

but it's mouth is inside out,
a pink, swollen bubble of cheeks like blown gum.

Every windshield along the curb line frosted.
Icicles baluster each chassis above the asphalt.

At the corner, a tailpipe exhausts and a brake light embers.
Their glass is steamed, the way the living

throw barriers against nature.
My own hands sweat in my coat pockets

and if I remove them
the skin cracks faster.

In Louisiana where my sister lives,
the bayou froze over,

something everyone she knew said would never happen.
The ice steamed as the sun rose,

and she said she could hear cracks run
across the frozen plates.

Under that same sunrise, I have no doubt
that in at least one alleyway in my city

at least one unfortunate soul by not waking
woke in some place he'll never have chance

to describe to anything living
and would have no language for if he did.

Every second of every day the universe dies a little more,
a light greater than any star diminishing.

I imagine I drift toward sleep in some hard place
where it smells of dirt, sweat, and tar,

listen to rats gnaw the edges
of old soup can lids.

The warmth trapped within layers of newspaper stuffed clothes
diminishes like coals in a camp fire

until the damp clamp of the world's breath
extinguishes the final embers,

and then, just as night reaches its darkest,
moonless moment, there;

the softest of cracks,
and then nothing remains

but a couple of jagged edges
for the soul to steam through.

Aeration

The fist of quartz with mica veins in the corner of the garden;
that is where the praying mantis croons vespers at dusk.
If I sit in one place long enough, everything becomes religion.

Bibles writ on parchments of cirrus, if I believe in the street lights,
I don't believe in the haze their light throws its body into.
A body isn't corporeal just because it is physical.

Otherwise, I would be my skin and what covers my ribcage.
This insufficiency rifles me. On my street alone, I am certain
that many candles sigh smoke tendrils, some burned to the stand.

Flicker gypsies dance atop pools of wax and pencil tips of blackened wick.
In the windows all across the skyline, ghosts resurrect in whiffs of perfume,
tinctures of tannins that linger, a brush of coarse fabric, and 10,000 tiny gods

birth in the hearths of the minds of the sleepers as lights go out.
Every second, the world re-weds, so in the honeymoon of starlight,
I learn how to strip clothing and keep my clothes.

At the Center of It

Something always keeps things from where they want to be.
Copper sheets keep slugs from gardenias,
nets the birds from the berries, and the roof bays the rain.

In the driveway, a ragged cat sizes up the trash bin—
smells the tuna cans, the scraps of salmon,
rotting chicken, turkey bones.

Every night, she sits and licks her chops, combs
her whiskers with her paw. Sometimes,
she hops to the top, scratches the smooth plastic,

not realizing that her own weight holds it shut,
just as in all things.   Lord, how I itch to step forward
and take hold of the railing, to make *something* happen,

But how I fear that if I do, nothing will.
Until then, the smell of cooling soil under wind
through dandelion stalks, rustle of wisteria leaves.

The soft click of a streetlight dowsing. Electric
buzz slips from the air like thread from a shirt.
The neighbor's dogs don't bark. All for me.

III.

1st Island Fisherman Mending his Nets

When I lie flat   on the dock
Over Raci Cove

And look down the slats

They stretch   infinitely
Into the sky

Water heard but not seen

I graze my cheek   on gritty planks
And listen

To boisterous screams of girls leaping

From the posts into the foamy
Current eddies

Wood rattle as the fisherman

Drops his lobster   traps
To dingy boat bottom

He doesn't know when he wafts

His net for one last   check
Of the twine

That he's casting to catch

The solar   flares
In his weaving

Earlier that day I saw him

Smoking hand rolled   cigarettes
On his porch

While he plucked the net strings

Like playing   a guitar
Lips pressed tight

He hummed the melody

His hands   did not make
Who knew

How ambitious his song.

A murder of eels

The night fisherman takes the eel by the tail,
swings its writhing body overarm like a hammer
and beats its skull against the concrete. Everything is
closed at this hour, so he holds its limp length up at me.
Needing to show someone. For there to be evidence.

Beneath the nightblack water, more eels
undulate against the nudges of the current.
Their slick sides grip the friction of motion
even though the fisherman gripped his catch
so tight, bones snapped like kicked gravel.

The undertow murmurs elegies until light winds
strum the bay into a tricklesplash of waves.
There is no way to hold the night still so late
because we only know what is by what comes,
the breeze a brush that cannot be brushed back.

In the graveyard at the edge of the bay

A candle in hand, my cousin Jenko spots me
perched on the flat edge of the tomb lid

pressing parchment against the stone
against the wind with the flat of my palm

to make a rubbing of the Cyrillic
on the graves at dusk.

Jenko in vestments came to light his candle
on the plot he will one day share

with his late brother above the bones of their father,
there, on the stone; his name already etched

under Tomislav, under Tomislav,
under Demitri;

wives stacked on wives, husband's on fathers;
families that dug their own mass graves.

On the mainland, they still stumble
across such sepulchres in out of the way places

that become the only way we should look
because we should not abide dusty corners

to live unswept in our souls
because orchards wither on a mountainside

and a village without children
in the streets is still more than interstellar medium.

This type of place knows
how much deeper the land than wide,

that the dust of a parent's bones
should cradle their child's

so when the resurrection comes
mother already holds son in loving arms;

so when the cold wind's cessation
coins a silence

and the blood moon rises off the mountain
to vomit hollow light onto the orchards

the figs don't wither on the vine
and every roots knows

no amount of living
teaches respite to the night.

Nothing is just itself when shadow
falls upon it, graves

the shadows of the dirt exhumed.
Their seeds dribble from our mouths

into our velvet lined selves
where they thirst among all our softness

as scorpions scurry from holes
among the stones

to await the dust of more bones
to grow like clay in the mist.

Glimmer

I.

Needlefish weave wakes
in   and out   of posts   to sew
            pier to sea

Crabs on rocks
            must think sideways

because forward is not constant   to eyes on stalks
            scuttling into concrete cracks

      Most times   I just glimpse
            from eye corners

And then forget
      the way someone remembers
            something   that never was

II.

The trawling net   of the Milky Way
                  (Algol)
            (Proxima Centauri)
                  disappears (Zeta Sadatoni)

over either horizon   like a belt that cinches the earth
                  into the sky

and I still can't perch   (snapper)   on the pier's edge
                  feet over fish (Chestnut Goby)
      (sand sole)   with grandfather's ghost   (spotted pipefish)

(mend his nets and paint the slats of his boat
            she'll survive at least one more trip round the cove)

and forget that it is easy to romanticize a man I hadn't seen
for eighteen years before he died

        and that the galaxy (Pegasus)
                        drags the stars
    (Cassiopeia)
      with such apparent   ease (Orion)

(Andromeda)   and the constellations
     formed by   the constellations
        breathe   with history

III.

The eels buck
     silt into thunderheads
and a dead sepia   withered and eaten by ocean churn

floats against the posts long before its season,
     where the blenny nip
     the flecks of flesh that   drift   off

I hadn't spoken to him   since I was old enough to understand
that a life I called simple
     could quickly turn brutal,

that he abused my mother   fist and belt,
     left red and black welts,
        down her legs and back,

that the calluses of his hands
        came from more
than dragging in the nets.

Destination

No human light invades this recess in the shoals,
  gas station light clouds, bar neon nebulae in evening fog,
  traffic signal red and yellow suns
  the galaxy of skies over elsewheres.

Here, the star chart maps my skin in the bluish whites
  of the pale flesh around the hearts of the fish
  that pip at whatever flotsam bobs the shore ripples
  as I watch satellites caress atmosphere.

Their light doesn't disturb the air it kisses,
  does not have feathers or pressing lips
  to whisper like the tides,
  but they tell me, you are there

on your back among the low churn of waves withdrawn.
  The ocean gives by taking away.
  The sea urchins that congregate on the rocks
  thrust up needles like hands in supplication

beg the wives, the children, the inspirations,
  the continuities to stop drifting off by inches,
  implore the moon to let down her gathered tidal robes
  and cease her stride toward the cosmos.

Don't leave us leaves us an empty nest of sky,
  they say, don't skim past pulsars
  and dwarf stars building a shell of ice
  in search of something to shatter against.

Requiem

I've buried   my grandfather here.
Old bricks crumble,   roofs slough tile,
mortar dust   drifts   lazy on wind.

Sitting against   his grave,
star clouds and village lights
shimmer on tourmaline bay ripples.

Skin against stone,   the letters
trace an epitaph on my back
in a language I can't understand.

Moored mast lights   distant beacons
blink codes   on the horizons.
Like they're talking   to the stars.

Until recent centuries, the world thought heaven loomed
beyond the solar system.   That souls
drifted up   on the lift of angel hands,

and star charts plotted the course of history.
Maybe   we've learned since then.
If I watch the stars long enough,

I'll learn a whole new vocabulary.   Just not
the one   that they speak.

Listening for Veles

I.
The shepherd broke his crook because too late he learned his flock was
made of goats, and the cattle dried into sheets of leather in the sun.
Little more than parchment and pit, grapes drop from branches into dust
and pebbles to be eaten by rats, pecked by gulls.
On a long, flat rock, a horned serpent lazes.

II.

Wind lick in hollow fork of oak root,
root fingers thrust into soil,
knuckles of knots in the sun,

last year's leaf mulch shelters worms and other soft
bodied things that tune the world
in a language of effluvial tremors.

III.

Draught's been too long for figs to plump.
Sometimes all you pick are wasps in skin.
Only so much water boats can haul each week.
The kids leave to Zadar for school
and city jobs and never come back.
Their beds are still made under all the dust.

IV.

Where is Perun in the clear sky?
Is there no lightning against the sun?

When will an eagle sit the branch
instead of gull and crow?

Dogs gnaw cobs in the landfill
and fish choke on flotsam in the cove.

V.

They believe that once these islands were a trail of step stones
that hopped the Gods between the living world and under
to the water where the snappers schooled before their call
to wavelets who speak the language of rain on leaves
and spray on pier posts laced with thunder trembled cracks
droplets pulling into roots where snakes coil in their dens.

On Recording a Dying Culture

Everyone who dies
without children
is the last
of a lineage
that traces
to prokaryotes.

A billion years
to grow
a set of bones
that bleaches
white in the sun
in less than one.

Long before then
the rats and wild
dogs will gnaw
out the marrow.

Sometimes,
one chokes,
adds its sticks
to the mix.

IV.

Becoming invisible

The street glistens rain
                and oily white pools of
              gull droppings
                    swirl

Beyond the low churn
              of wavelets
                    from Sarika cove

Below droplets
                dimple the sill

There
          a full-bellied laugh
              from a round-bellied woman

The cobblestones lift a mist as if they refuse wetness

I turn from the light
          and my body becomes   invisible

In a dark room
         skin is contoured
            shadow

Without my eyes
            whatever I see
           becomes what is
               even if
                    I can't show anyone

I close my palm
          around the ball
          of a laugh

sit at the desk
          with my elbow next to the old touch-tone phone

I promise

I will set the receiver off the hook

so the darkness can speak
    to the no one on the other end

What I swallow

The butcher wipes his blades then
      drapes his display with bacon
            still warm from the pig.

Tapeworm larvae writhe through pork,
      and no one on the street speaks
            a language I understand.

Their word for eggs gathered from the left
      of the henhouse differs from the word
            for eggs on the right.

There is no common diction for the heart.
      We cannot describe the pulse   of ventricles
            and what they pump in the same breath.

In accordance with such uncertainty,
      on either side of a door,
            a pair of olive   women

sip black tea from wooden mugs.
      I do not know   at what they look
            if I know they look left.

Inside, simple fare. Bread. Boiled eggs. Ham medallions.
      The table of my soul,
            empty chairs near and across.

The brunette

Outside the church you
        hunch on the stone bench.

The last of an evening mist
        clings your dress

to your knees and pulls them
        together

as if the damp cloth doesn't want
        you to have more children.

Watch the prowling currents of cats
        under the grace of starlight

sifted through shifting schools
        of leaves

until you hear one kill
        or rather hear what is being killed

make its presence known
        one last time to the darkness.

Gaze down and to the right
        as if you remember being lied to.

Your face the lovely that only
        looks right if there are tears on it.

I would wipe them away
        were they there,

If I were there
        and not just a man

who finally noticed someone

they hadn't known

was in the frame
  when they snapped the photo.

I do remember that just after
  the shutter closed,

Eleven tolled the steep bell
  as if to say

we've all been lied to
  to the cats, to the bench, to God,

and now we both wait,
  other to each other,

for night to devour us
  and the church doors in morning

to fling open and
  spit out our bones

Walk

Toward the graveyard we walk
        sun on the slender Sarika Cove shore
so few clouds so few graves ahead

This land is not abundant
        slopes segmented into eighths acres
for the old vineyards, long dried

There is no native mammal
        just birds and what
stowed away in the hulls of water haulers

Rain can't replenish this land
        and we clasp
sweaty palms our conversation intermittent

splashes of bold white   fish
        the slap of waves
against rocks our words–

we don't share enough language for me to
        explain whose graves I wish to visit
How can we express ourselves

properly in nouns? How
        do you teach
loss without what is not there?

Hearing the cuckoos cry

With you in my arms, I long for you to be in my arms,
for barriers of skin and soul to collapse.
Your chest presses mine as if your breasts
fill my lungs. Just as far away, black holes dance

amid colliding galaxies. Event horizons kiss.
Two dimensions, neither the one we share,
pour into each other like a waterfall pouring
against a waterfall that flows upward.

Not even time survives such torrent.
Quantum froth. A pulverized atom spray
and shattered energy constituents.
Roaring loss of fusion, inverted stars.

In that new place between, there must be
a placid pool where everything rests.
We spin naked in cool, radiate rings.
Reap the softness from each other's hair.

Road up the mountain

Succulents and cacti

    blue flowers   among needles

On a rock   a gila monster suns
    maybe sentinels for flies

    or mice.

I wouldn't pretend to know   what it wishes
    filled its armored belly

    or what such a soldier would conquer

It opens mouth to hiss
    without messy valiance

mesas on one horizon wobble painted ribbons   in heat mirage
    sky flat as an ocean twinkles with high birds

Eyes that gaze without a hint of soul

    tail buckles   flexes

and between those teeth

    storm clouds slide out.

Getting it right

Let's look at it this way:
we are shepherds on the hillside.
Maybe we are at leisure with our crooks
rested at our feet, and finger perhaps a flute
or a scrap of paper, forgetting the sounds
of cities, pumping engines, chains clanking,
crane hydraulics extending wrought hooks.
We don't remember the color of sirens
or the sound of police lights, and attempts
to recall bring more clover on the wind,
succulents flowering on the hillside just up
the path from the well. Soon, it will be time
to lower the bucket, to think towards
tending the fire. While the sheep stir
in the pen, we'll stir the coals with iron.
In a timid kindling glow, a lamb crying softly
through one window, one of us will look
to the other and say, We've been going
about this gig all wrong. If we castrate a rat,
and tie a bell around its neck, sheep will follow it.

Godwin's Law

is the statistical correlation between an increasing
number of participants in a conversation
and the likelihood that one of those participants
will compare the topic to Hitler.

Therefore, swine flu? Hitlerish.
Drug users? Hitlerites.
Sightings of the Virgin Mary?
Hitlerism at its very worst.

Thus were born cupcakes that are like Hitler,
those blond cakes identical in muffin trays,
Hitleresque albino squid among shoals
feeding on water flotsam.

One day, you and I will share
a Hitler-style sunset
from the Straza Hitlertop.
We'll be Hitlered

by a sudden breaking storm
and find ourselves drenched
and laughing
at the Hitlereousness of it all.

All that lasts

The Maestro Wind conducts wavelets into the cove
where they play celesta on the rocks while
goats bleat from the mountainside

Stone walls segment the mountainside
baritones of form
that sever figs from vineyards and vineyards figs

Been years since the cistern dried
its cement eye on the mountainside
when the rain stopped its applause

and my grandfather bowed
just bones in a casket under dirt below
where goats bleat legato on the mountainside

Few of the villagers remember who owned the groves
and no one knows who named the cove

so they nod off
in their boats
to the sinfonia concertante
and dream of raisins and pits

I say
       let the goats bleat
       Let them lock horns

stamp hooves and cloud the dust
tumble rocks from terraced vineyards
staggered up the mountainside

The Goats Have Taken Over the Barracks

I.

Fifty years later, she-goats lie on their sides in the rotting cots
of the barracks,
bellies exposed to help the army of kids reach nipples. Each nurses
      each other's young when several
         give birth around the same time. A collective soul
of motherhood, and the same mothers cluster together months afterward.

There were blankets and pillows at one point, but now only a few gray tufts
      and grayed tufts
         of white stuffing remain.
And an occasional thread that hovers in a sunbeam
      three feet off the ground.
Where are the wires? Where are the wires, and what tethers we can't cut.

II.

Eventually, the groups of mothers   drift   apart
      their kids drift   farther, off,

        a magnetism failed.

        The bindings of all galaxies are tugged by the passing of distant
stars.
          The fabric of the shirt of the universe catches on brambles.

Are quasars the flowers between thorns the goats grind between their molars?

        One of a binary star will always devour the other.

III.

A dead bird. A rusty hooded jeep. Military issue with quadruple flats.
      Twenty-two caliber bullet holes

      in the emergency gas can

but no fire damage.

The driver-side windshield
is cracked in half.

The liquid part of the bird's blood has evaporated off the rusted metal.
        What is left stains the skin.

IV.

The mess hall. All the tables collapsed, the bench metal
        bowed to the floor. Part of the ceiling came
        down onto what used to be a buffet line of fold-out card tables.

The wood floors used to be buffed daily, a routine shared by English, Italian, and
Russian
        soldiers, a soldier routine shared by every military that ever occupied the
island, but,

now,

the pellets lie so thick and even across the mess hall floor footsteps
        give like they're on carpet. All the families
        of Ist Island cushion their own hardness.
                Crooked between the spurs
                of Mount Straza,

the diminishing of their memories is not like the fading floor varnish.
        It is an accumulation of forgettings.
        Burdened by thorns broken off brambles.
                The cousins forced
                        to cut each other's faces
                to save their fathers.
                When the soldiers shot
                        their fathers anyway.

The next day, when those soldiers

swapped stories
in the village
by the shrine to Mother Mary.

The   exact   notes   those soldiers laughed
as they described mothers' screams.

The way they echoed
off the cobblestones.

V.

The sand in the cove sheaths shards of bedrock.
The real face of the island would cut my feet
if I put my weight on it.

These same rock edges grow inside like bone spurs
on the hearts of the villagers. Their dreams are dock-post barnacled,
so thick with layered deposits I can't even tell
what was living about them.

The mothers here still bronze their children's first shoes
and light candles to the Virgin Mary at dusk
in memory of their children's fathers.

Given enough time
the blowing brine would eat all the wax away anyway.

When a child pulls a starfish out of the water,
how many tentacles reach from that pentagon spindle of mouths.
The way that they learn how long after starfish bites still burn.

VI.

Up the North mountain
to the barracks.

To artillery pits where I
        still
                read

        firing coordinates

        for both the east

        and west Adriatic coasts.

It doesn't matter if I don't want to
        read
                them

because I will have
        read
                them

before I realize
        what
                was
                        read,

That if I owned a sexton and binoculars,
I could line up the nearest target
        and see
through the living-room windows
        of six families depending
        on the decimal
                of my angle.

VII.

When I stand among all the ghosts of the guns
with the echoes of their recoils still embedded in the rocks
evoking the scent of hot copper,

I can still see where the barrels cast their shadows. How those shadows
swung with the rise, crest, fall of sun.

Stamp the world with the lithograph of my memories
as I listen to rocks fall away from the hoof of a goat.

VIII.

Every thirty feet between the emplacements' vomiting sandbags,
          a rectangular cement pit opens a mouth in the sand.

Reinforced concrete covers once sealed these pits
          against the possibility of enemy artillery.

I don't know who shattered the covers,
          but maybe they wanted to hear
                    what those mouths had to say.

Men would sit sealed in those pits,   wait to call coordinates
          through three inch tubes—sit-rep would echo from the emplacement
          into the pit,
                    sit-rep from pit
to command
about the emplacement—
                    the order from command
                    relayed back to the emplacement.
          Baton.

          Too much shrapnel in the air to do it any other way.

I imagine sitting in that dark chamber,
          sweat drenched and smelling it,
                    nothing to hold on to
          but the fight and what I am fighting for,
          knowing that when the battle comes
                    I will need to chose which is more important.
          Knowing which is and that I will choose the other.

That with a blade in my hand and the sun in my eyes
        a goat can be just a goat.

The pit is wide enough to turn a circle in
        without brushing elbows on the edges
                and still house small spiders in the corners.

        Who could crouch down and let them close the lid?

If the enemy did overrun the position
what they might send
                down the
                little
                black
                mouths
                of those tubes.

If I look into it, up real close   put my eye
        right up to it–

The last note

The water's not murky at night here though
the heart might be. The whistler at the pier's
edge sets tune to the whine of fishing rods
flinging line. Stars cry out their secrets
to the galaxy. Languages of flashes
and fades whisper of distance   and vacuum.
We would not think the stars were so constant
if they were always there. When winter slides in
on a south wind, white sands shift under
blue waters, colors of peace and ice,
coldness of space. Under the surface,
jellyfish drift, caress squid meat off hooks
with barbed tentacles and rising bubbles.
Once the whistling stops and the village
lights blow out, red snappers will swarm
the pier posts, following the scent of bait.

About the Author

Andrew Najberg teaches creative writing and other classes for the University of Tennessee at Chattanooga where he also previously served as the assistant director of the Meacham Writers' Workshop. His chapbook of poems *Easy to Lose* was published by Finishing Line Press (2007), and his individual poems have appeared in *North American Review, Louisville Review, Artful Dodge, Yemassee, Bat City Review, Nashville Review, Istanbul Review* and various other journals and anthologies. He is a winner of an AWP intro award in poetry and was a Pushcart Prize nominee.

Thanks to:

Art Smith
Kathleen Driskell
Matt Urmy
Richard Jackson
Earl Braggs
Alex Quinlan
Debra Kang Dean
Molly Peacock
Greg Pape
Marilyn Kallet
Jack Gilbert
Curt Allday

www.ingramcontent.com/pod-product-compliance
Lightning Source LLC
Chambersburg PA
CBHW021158090426
42740CB00008B/1150